European Girls

Hot Sexy European Lingerie Girls Models Pictures

By **PHOTO ART LOVER**

Copyright © European Girls

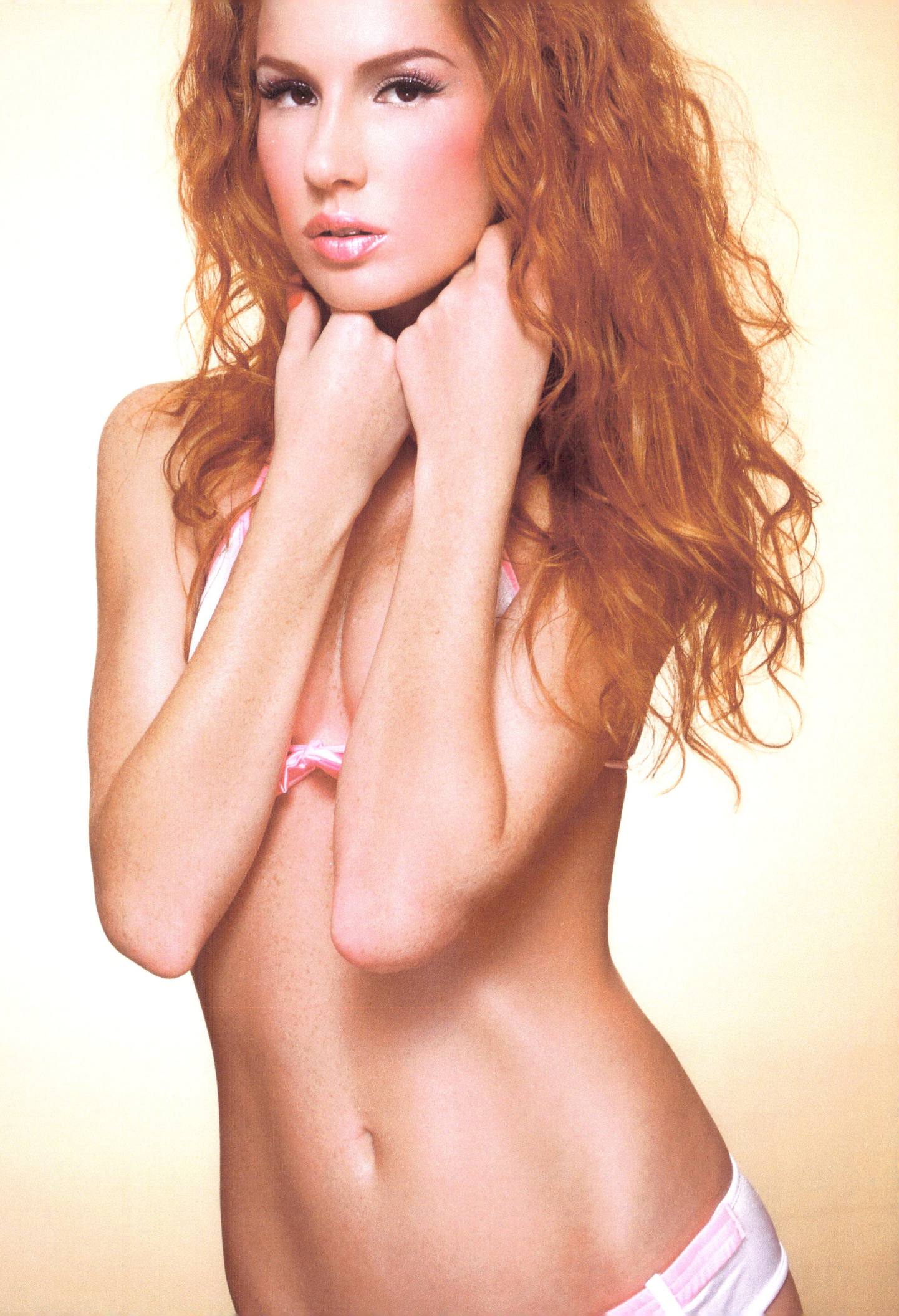

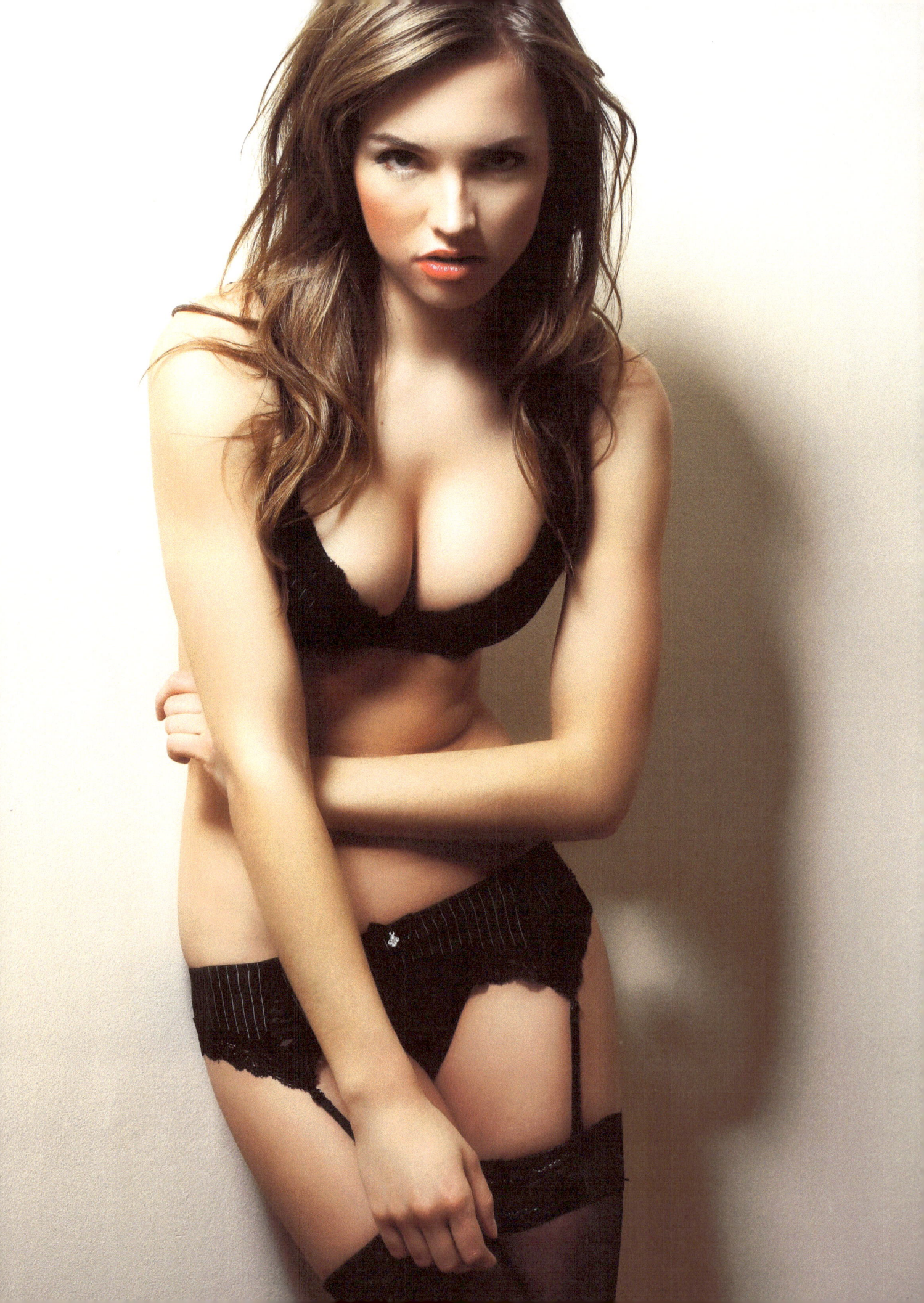

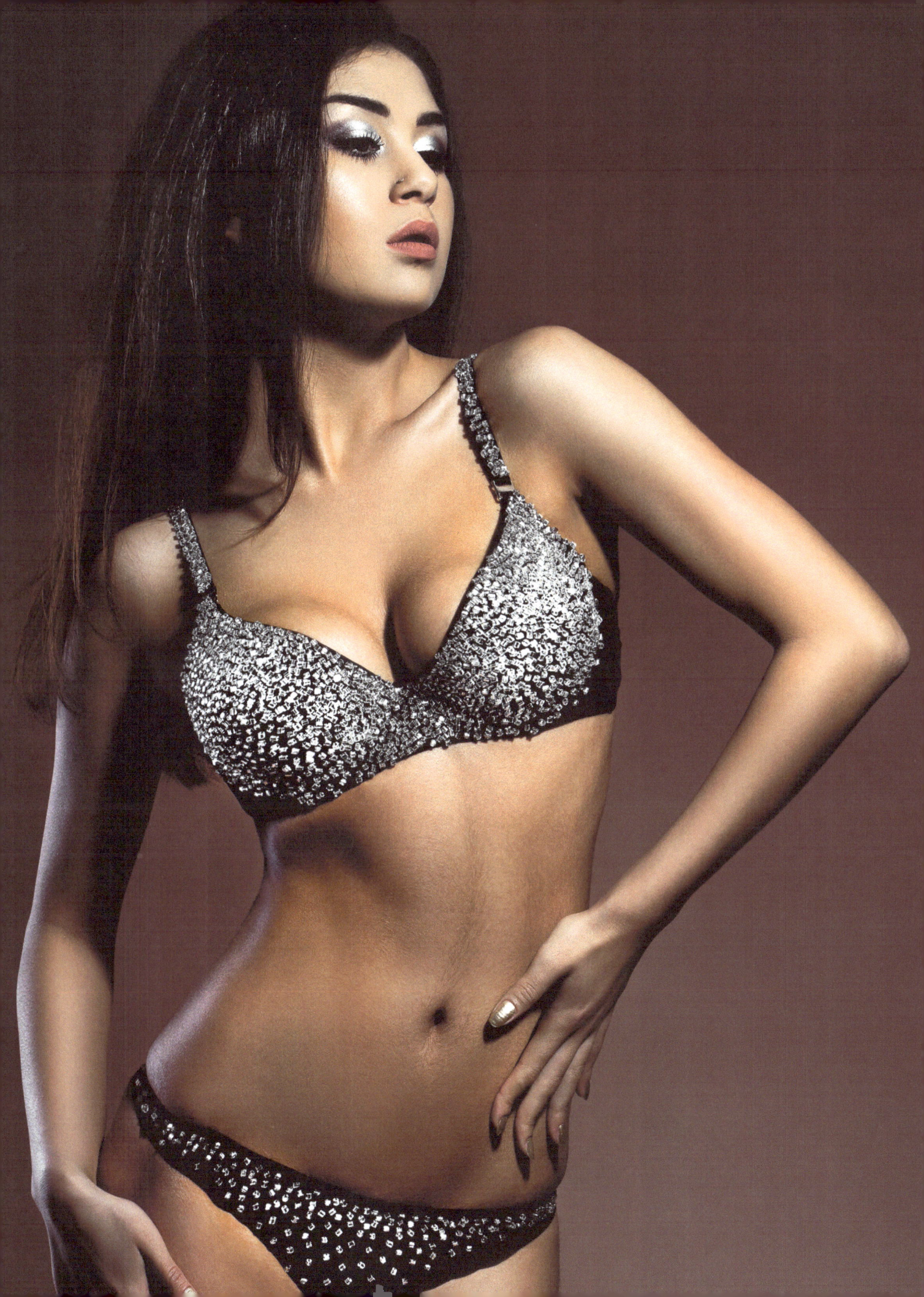

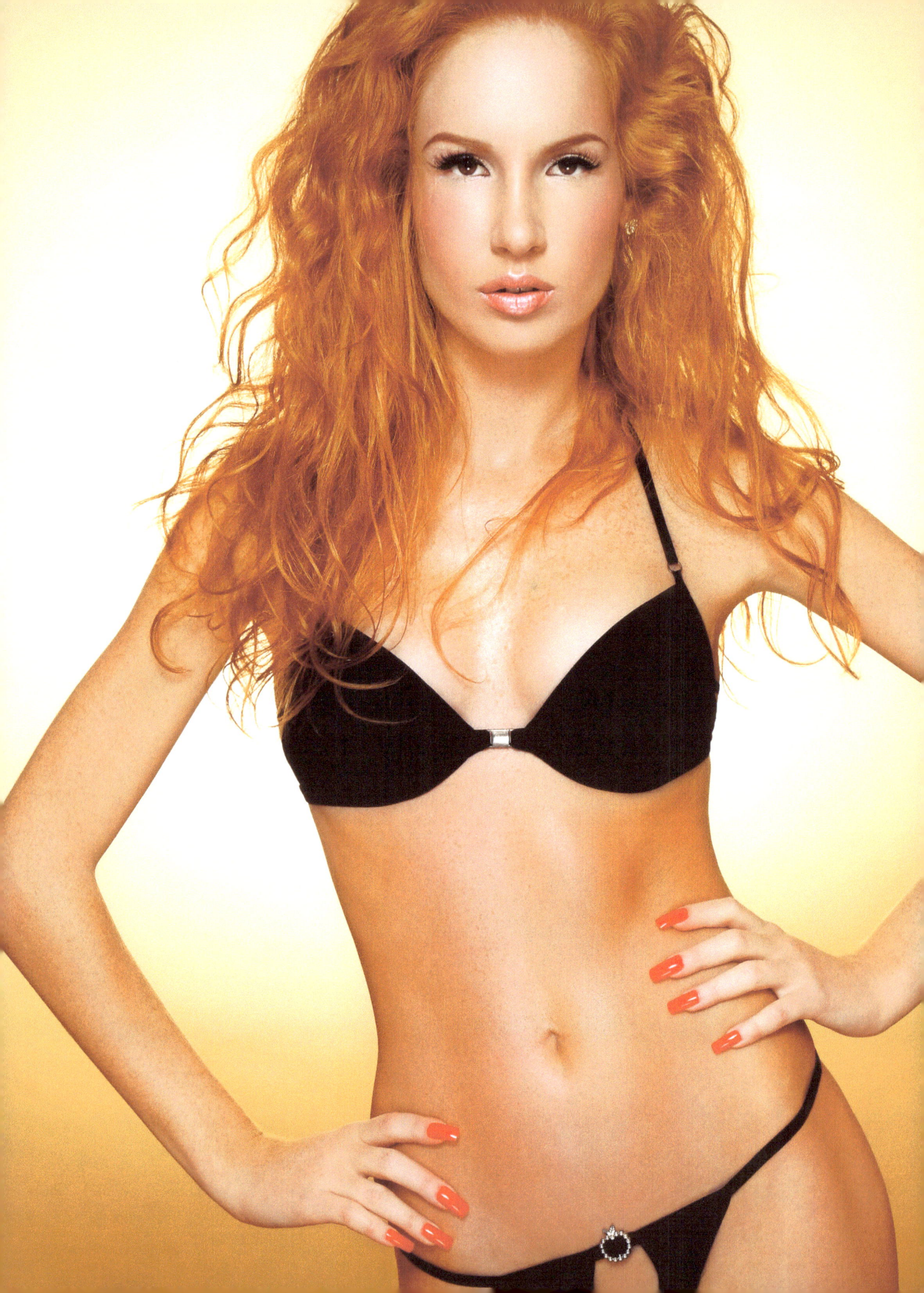

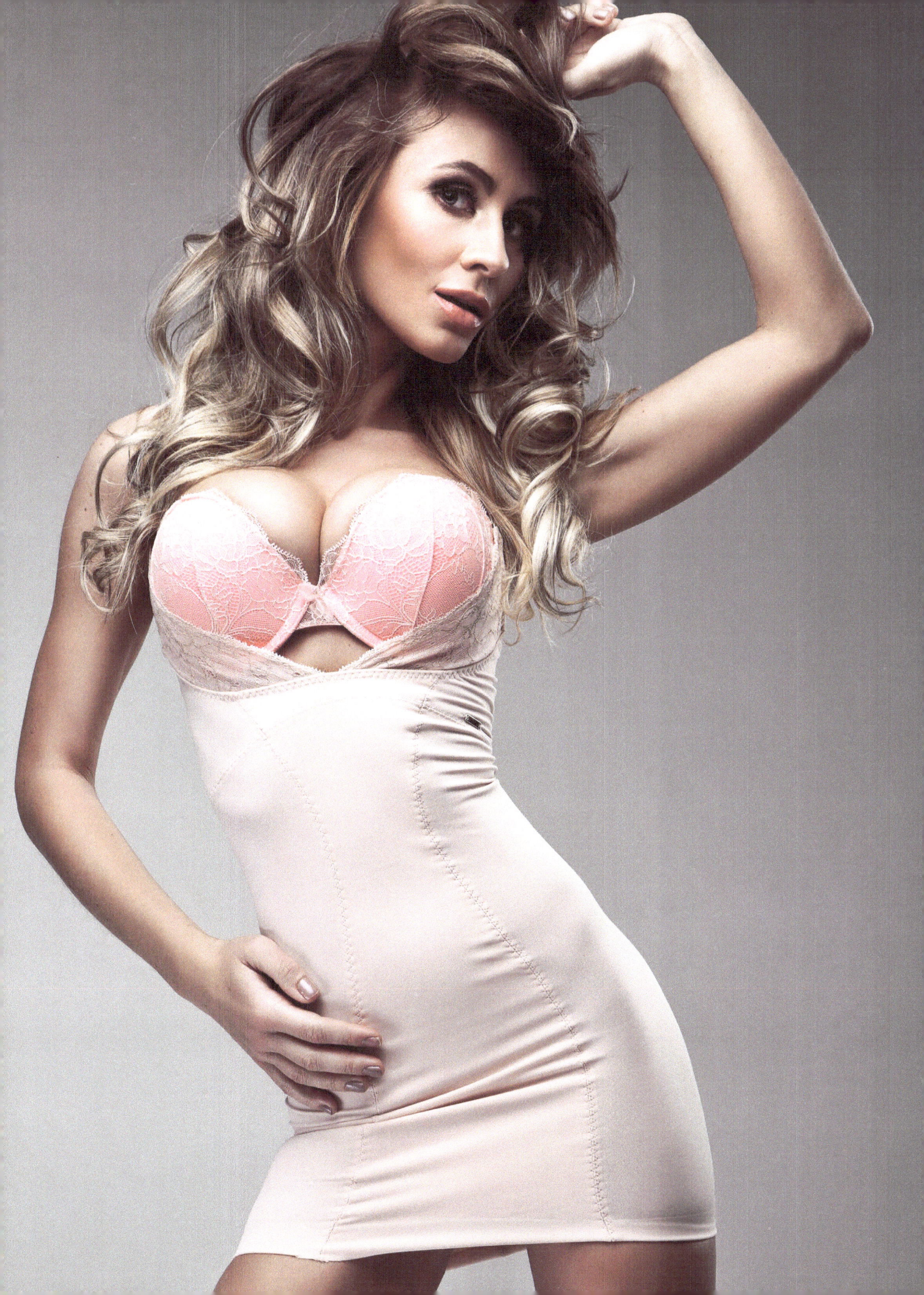

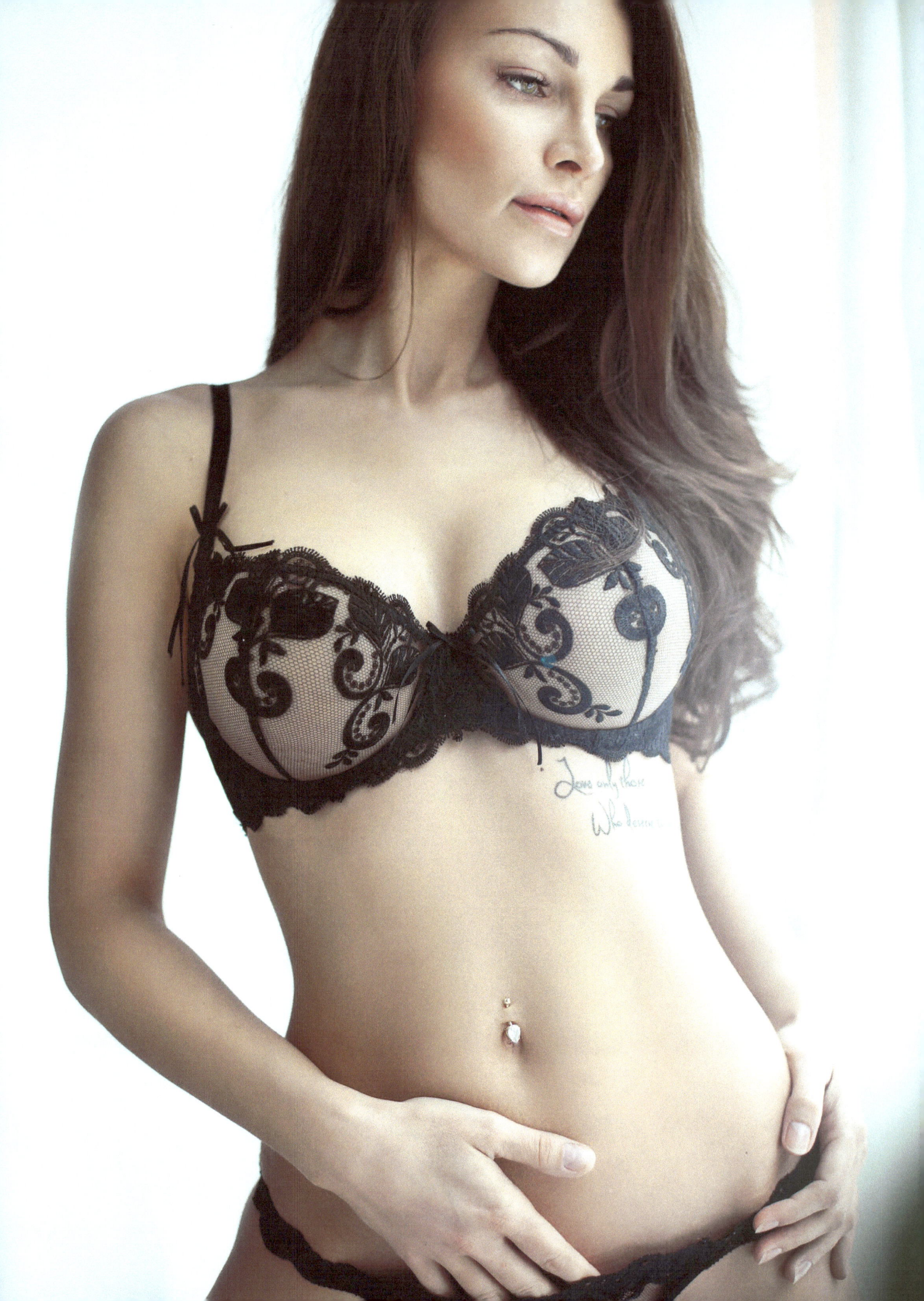

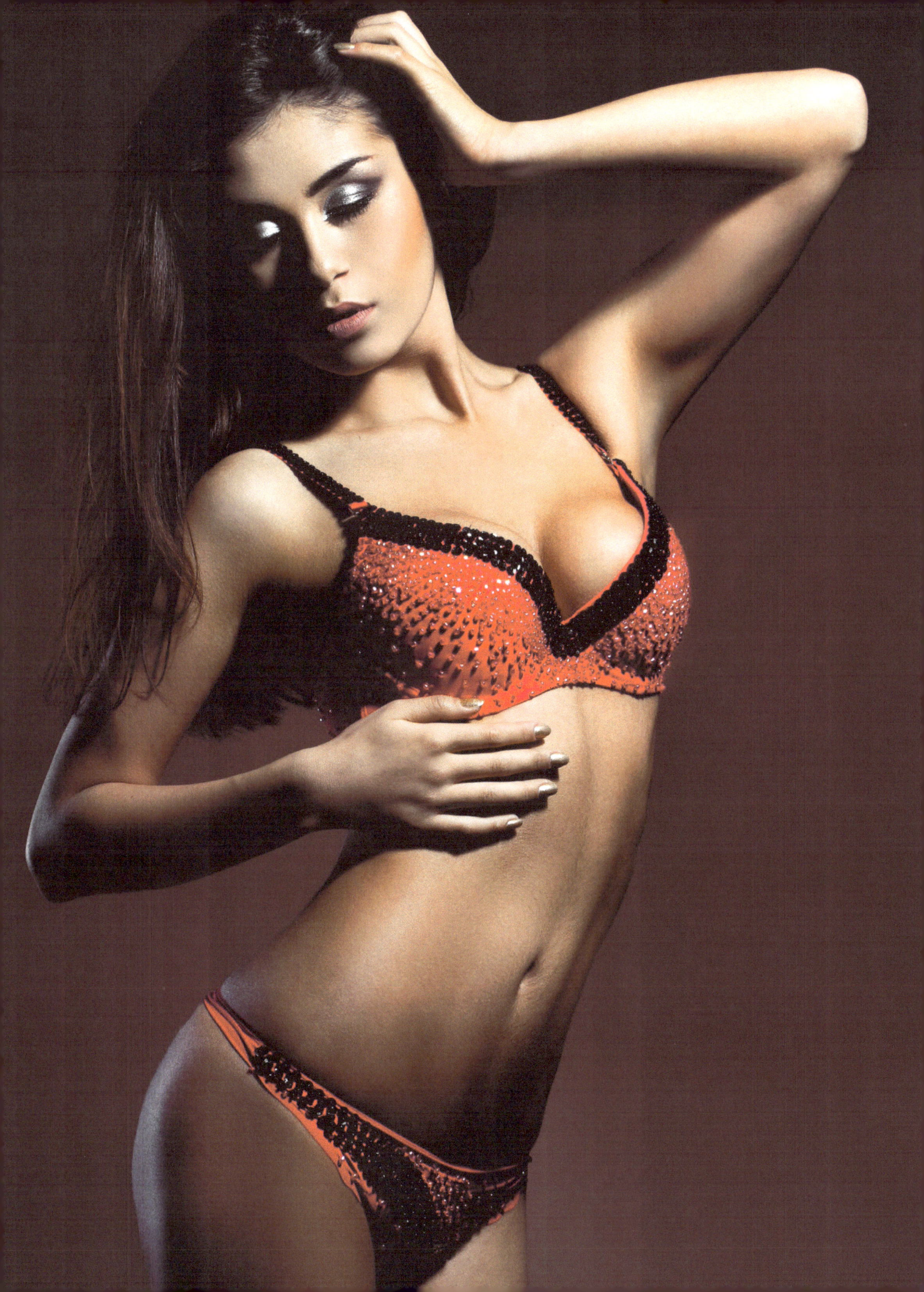

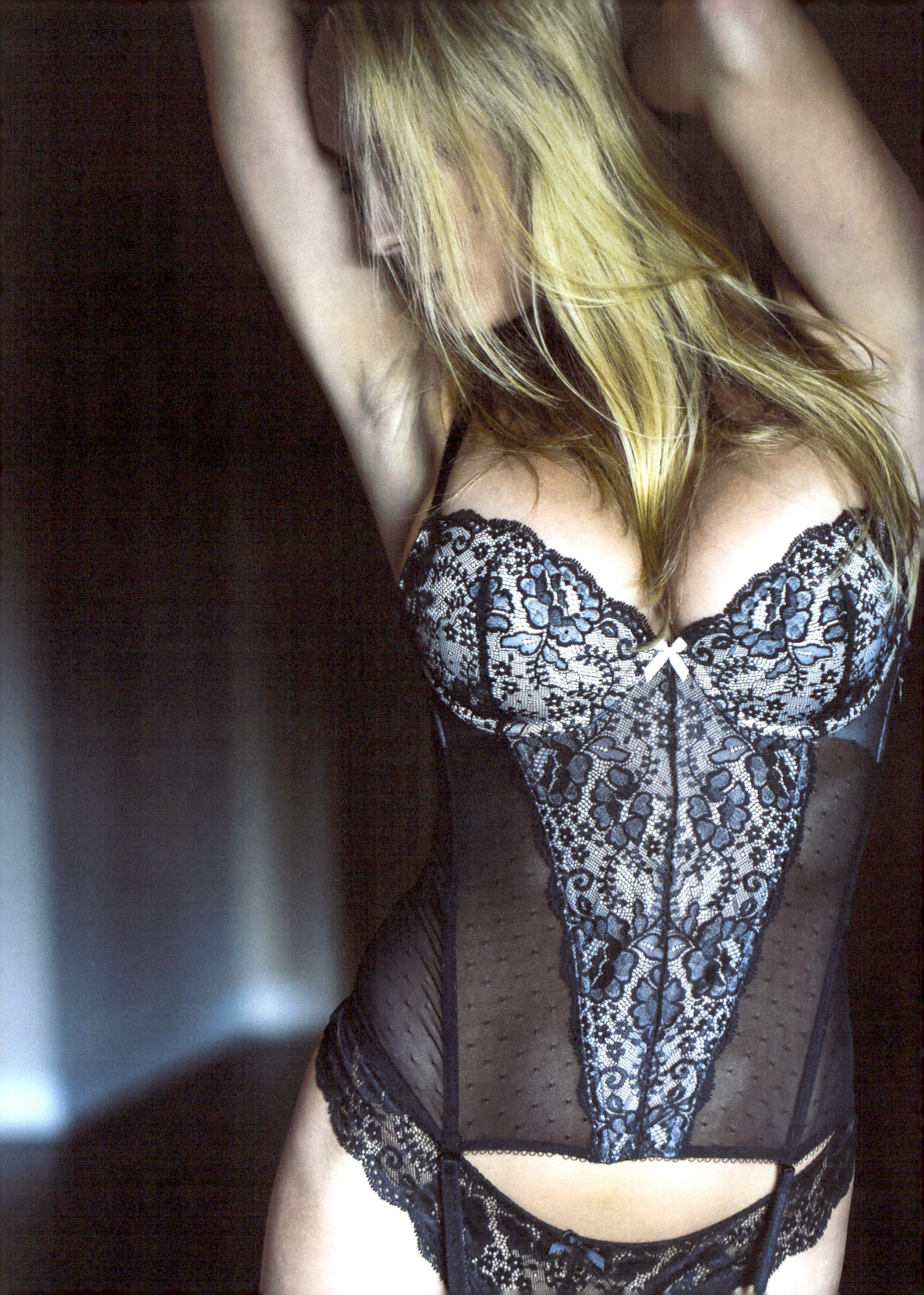

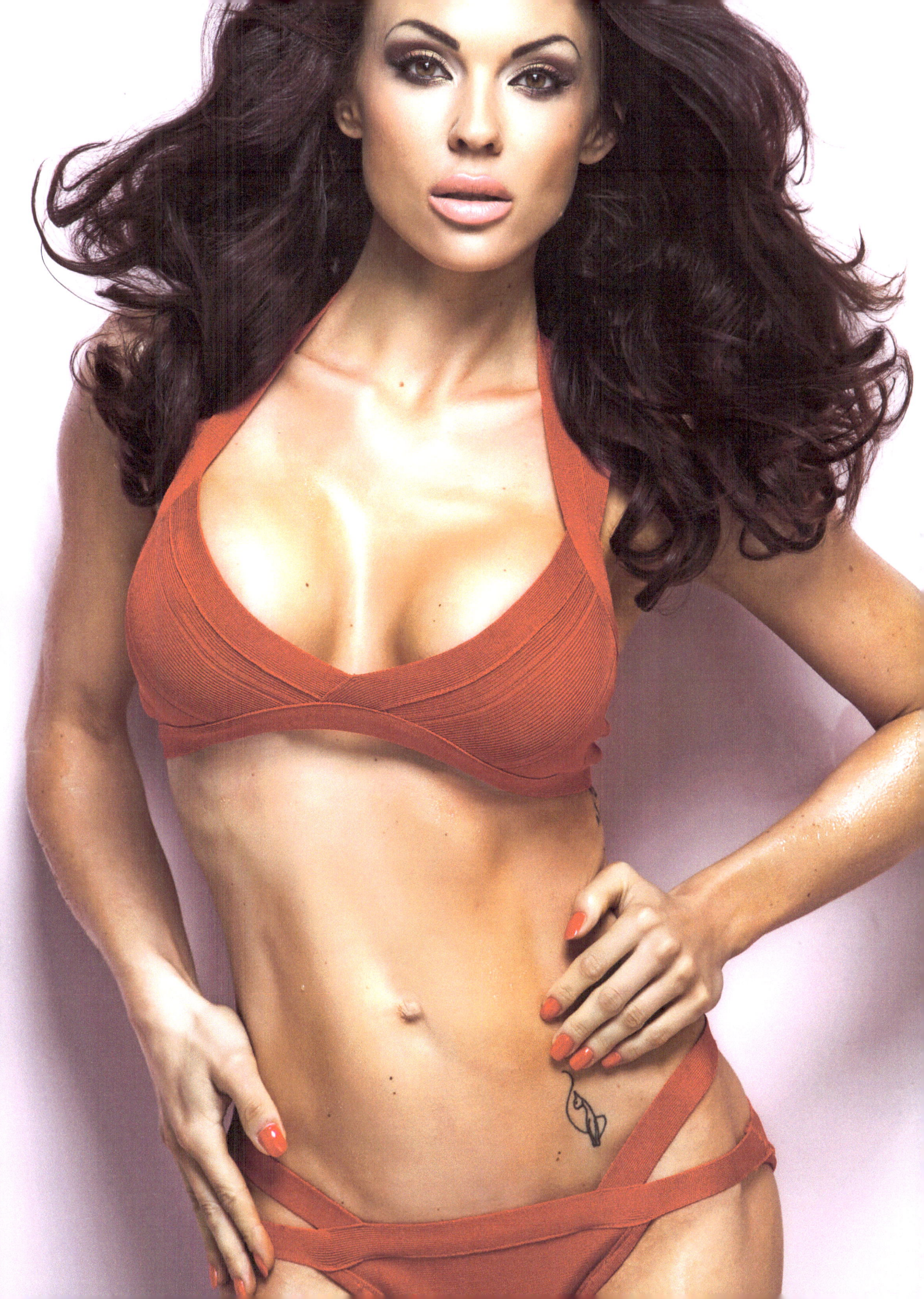

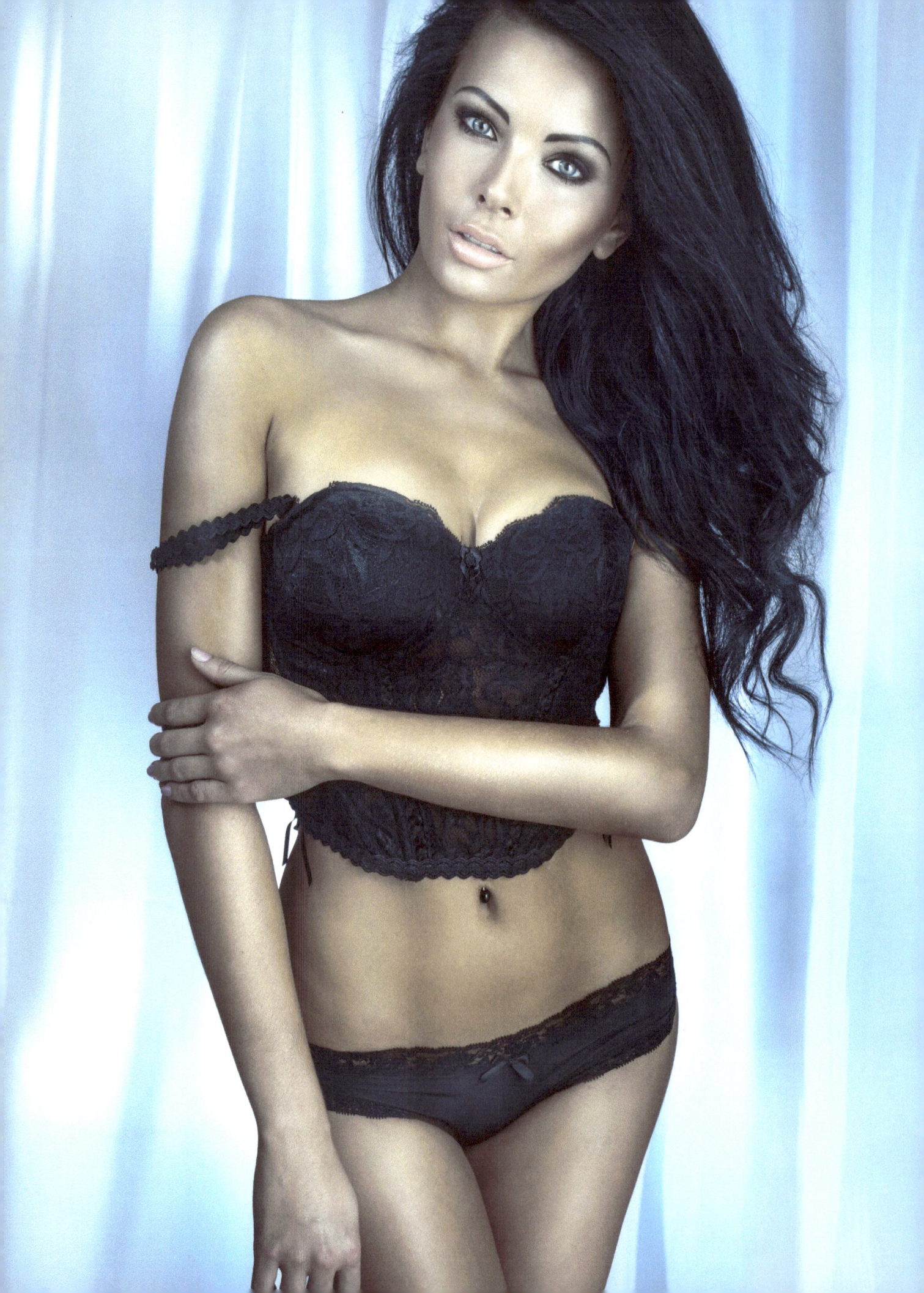

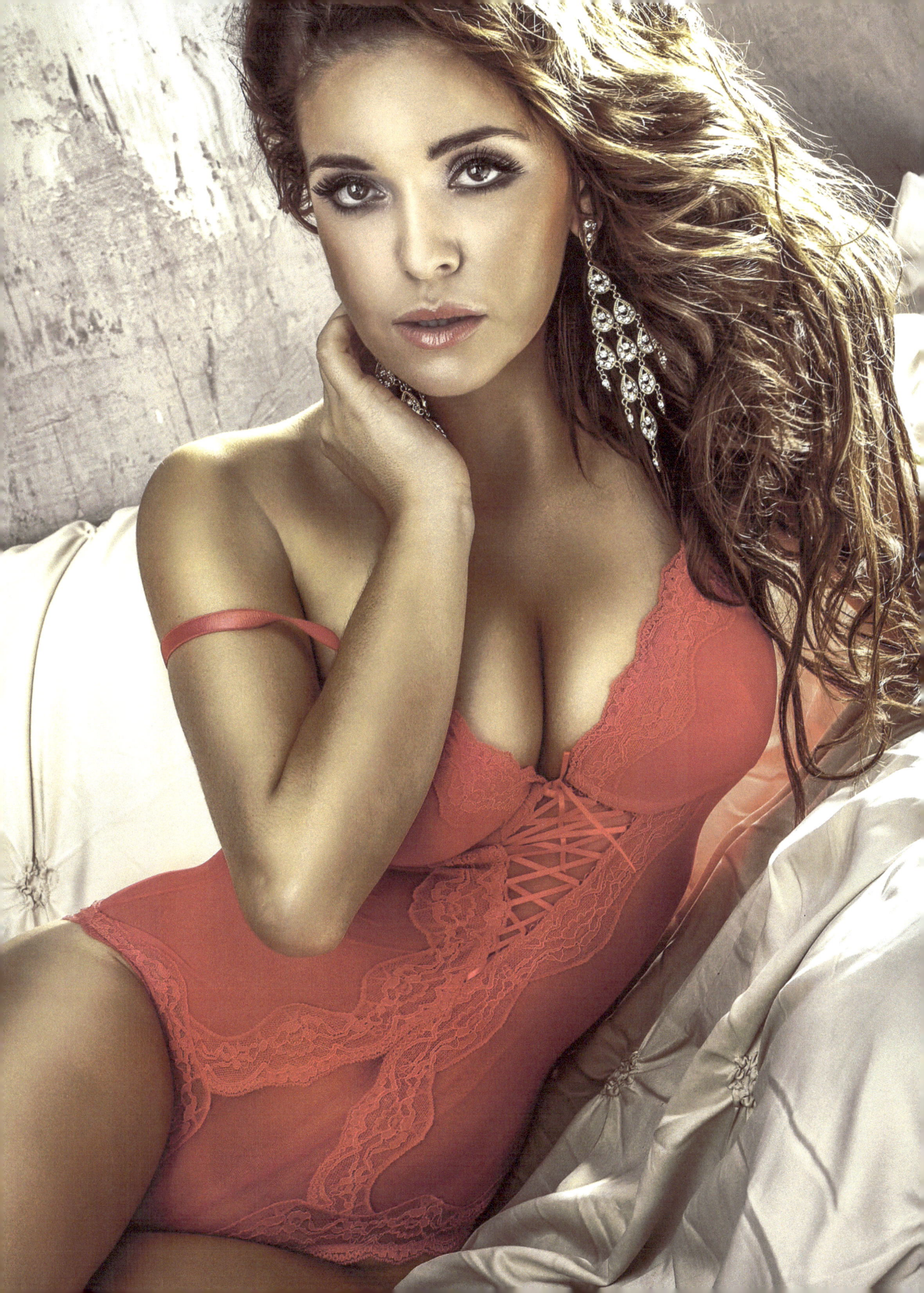

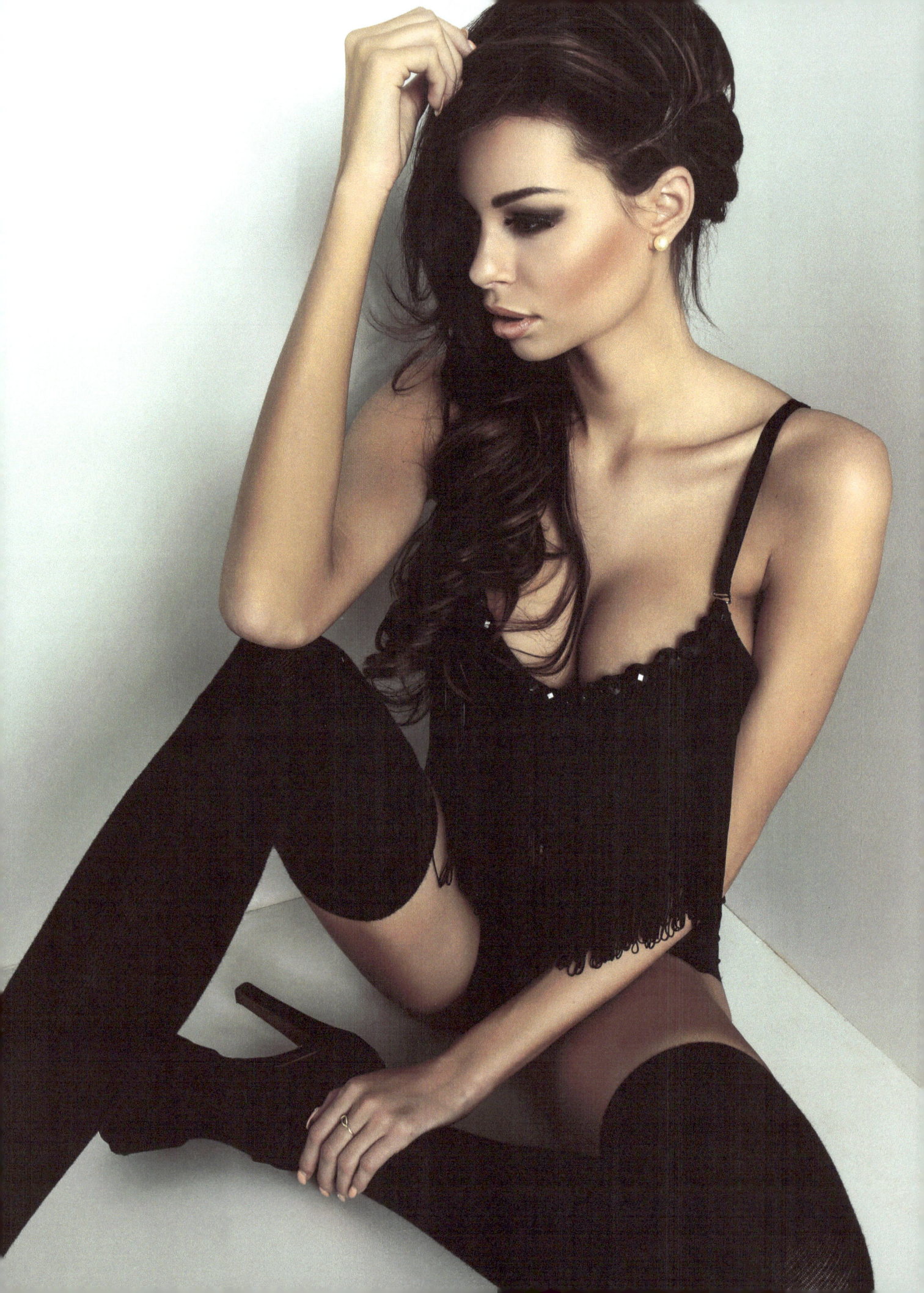

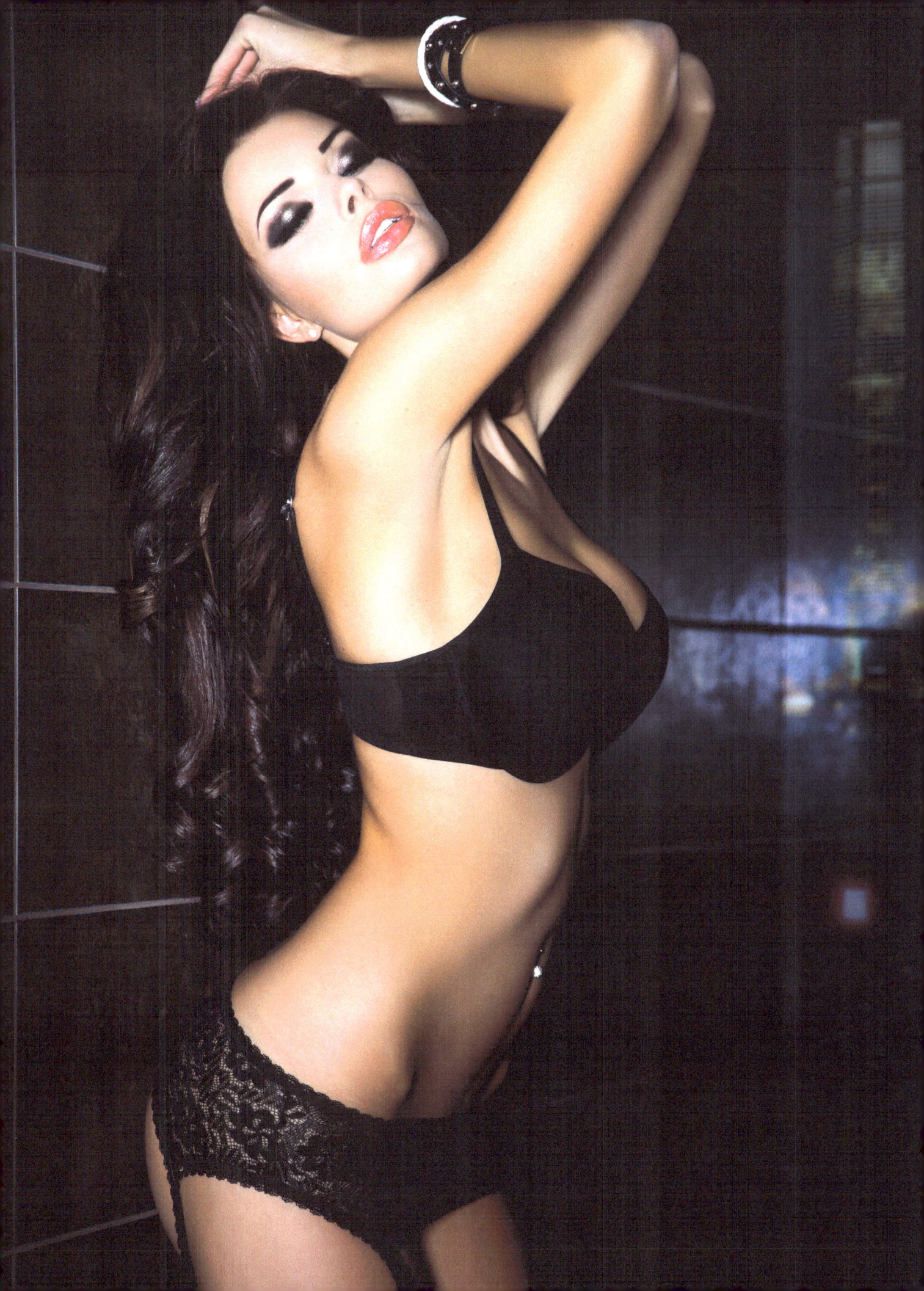

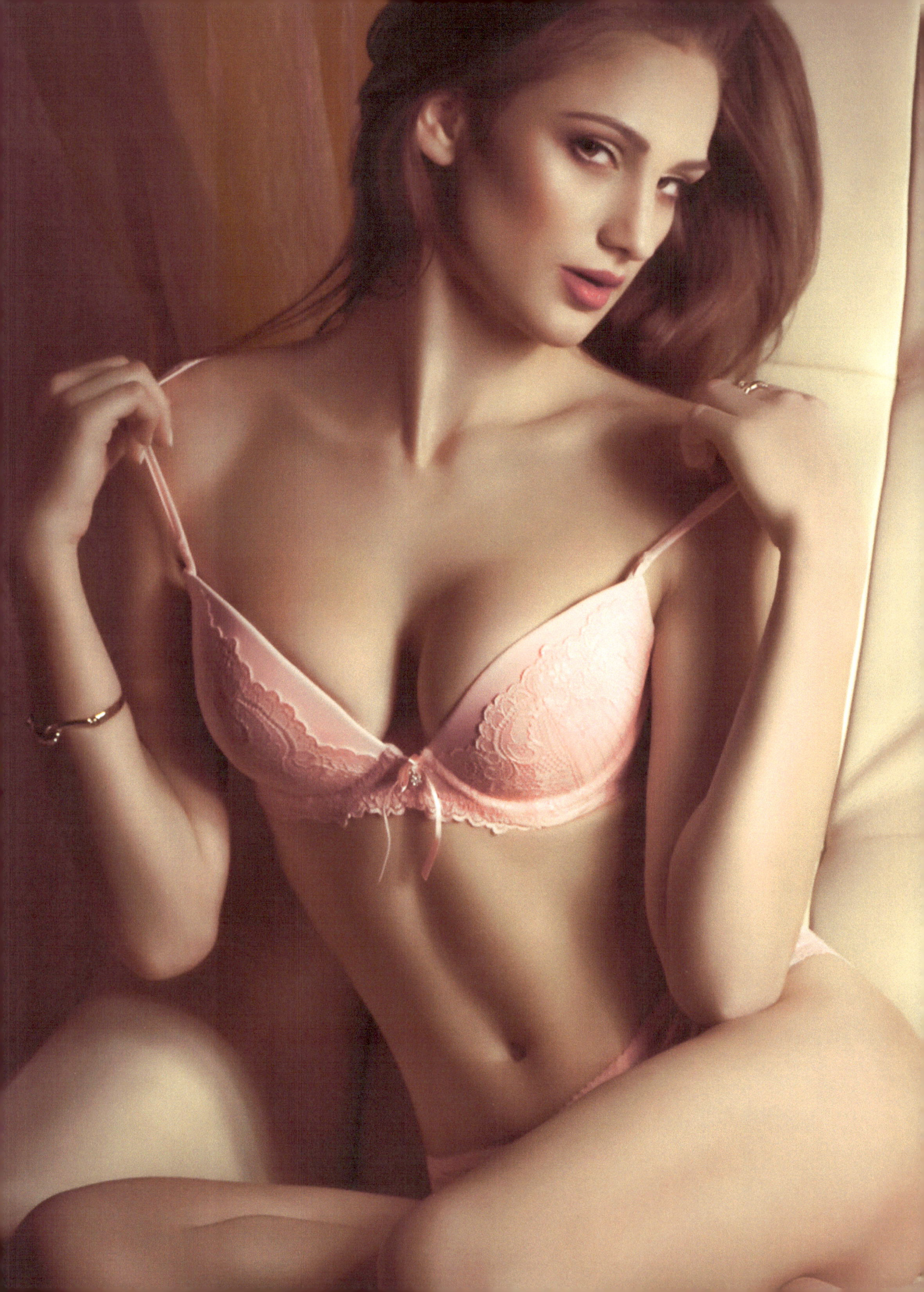

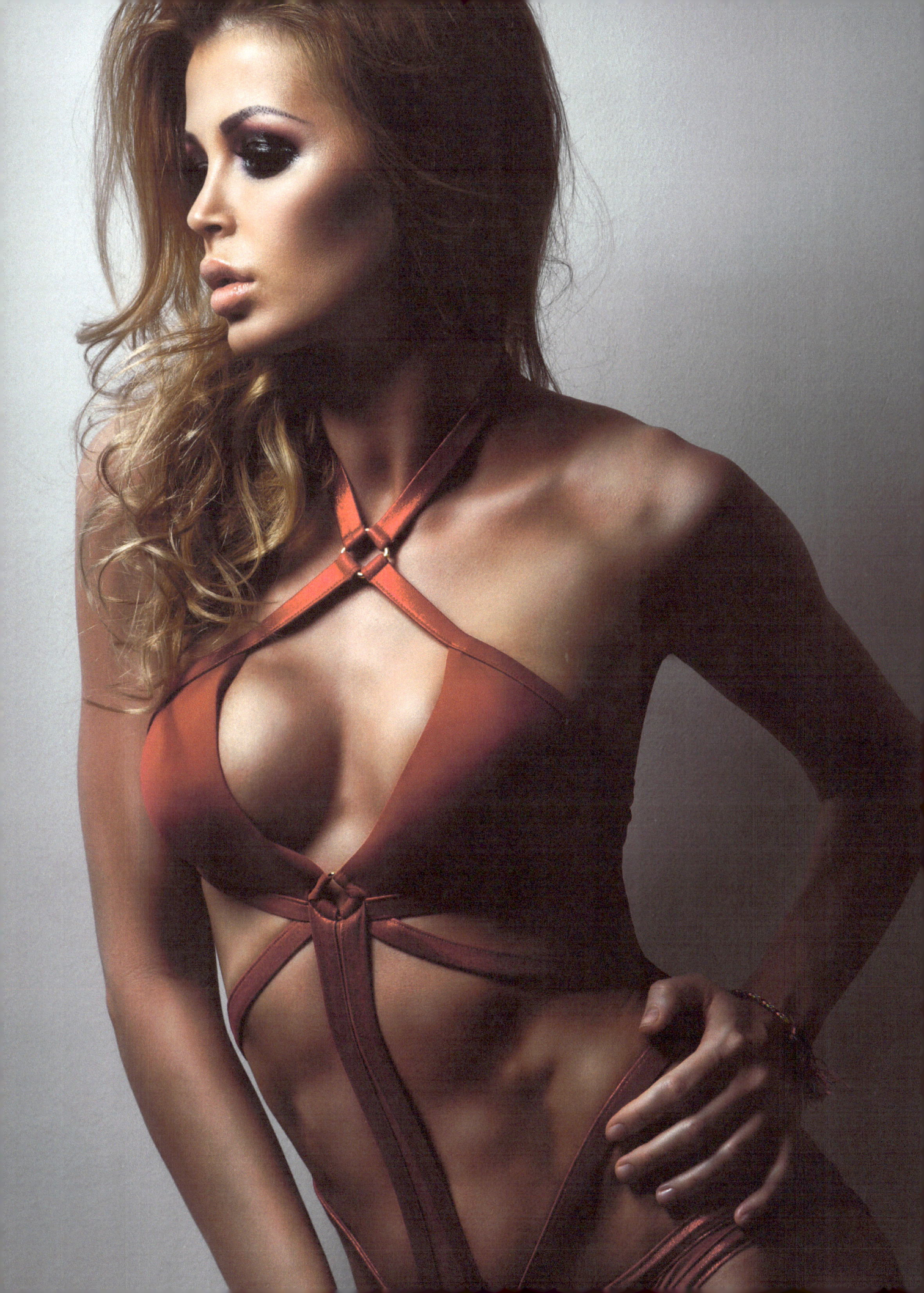

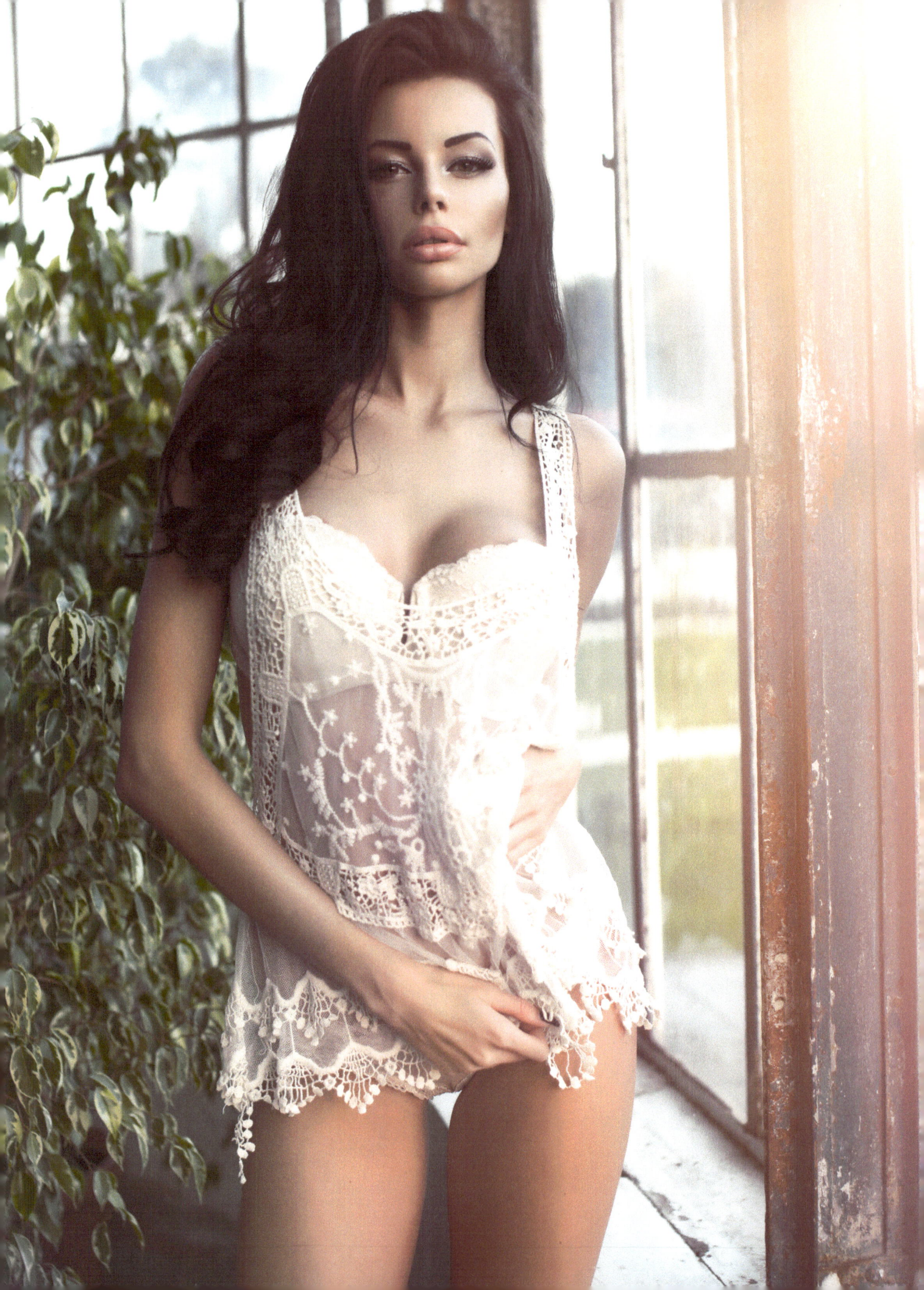

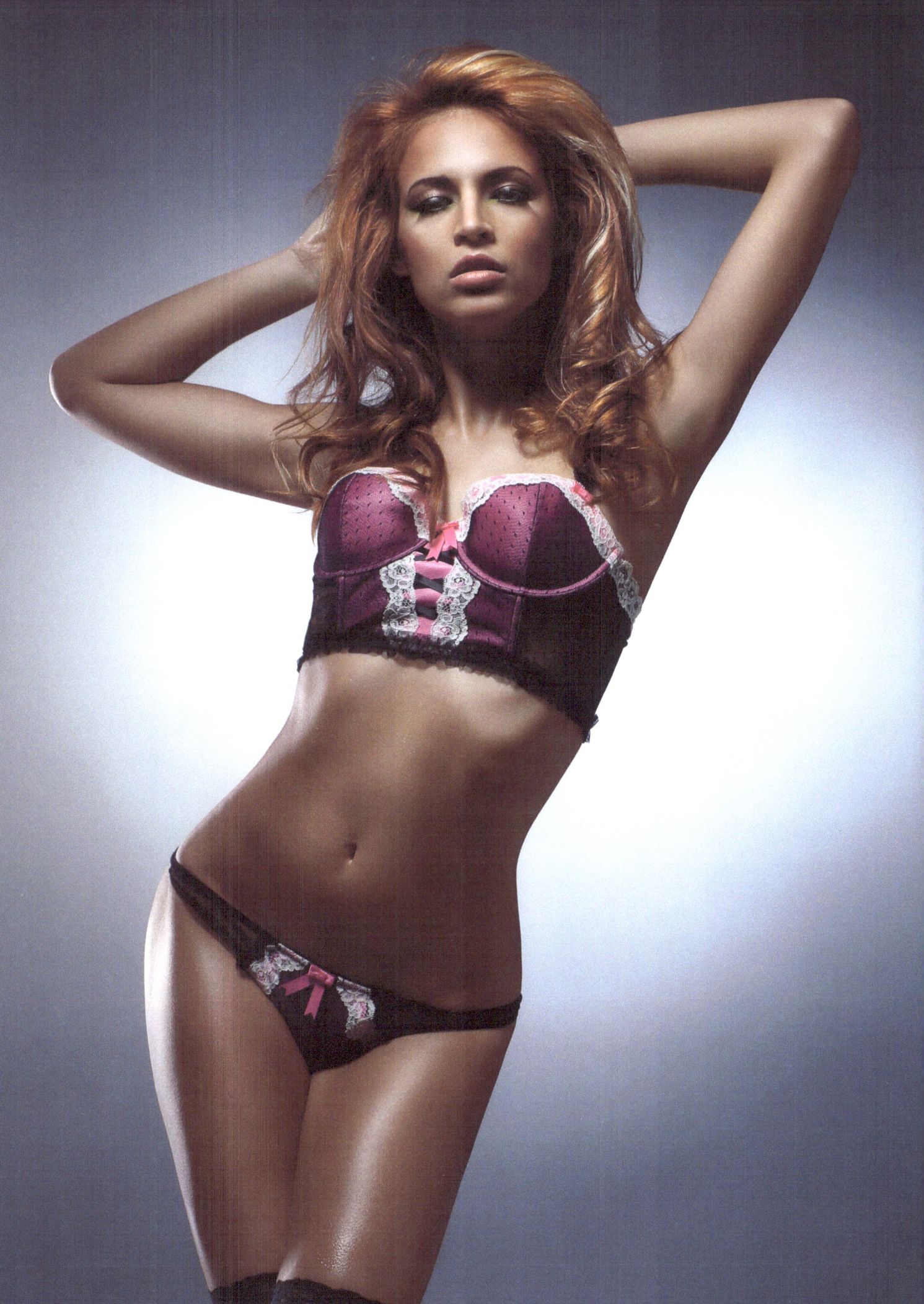

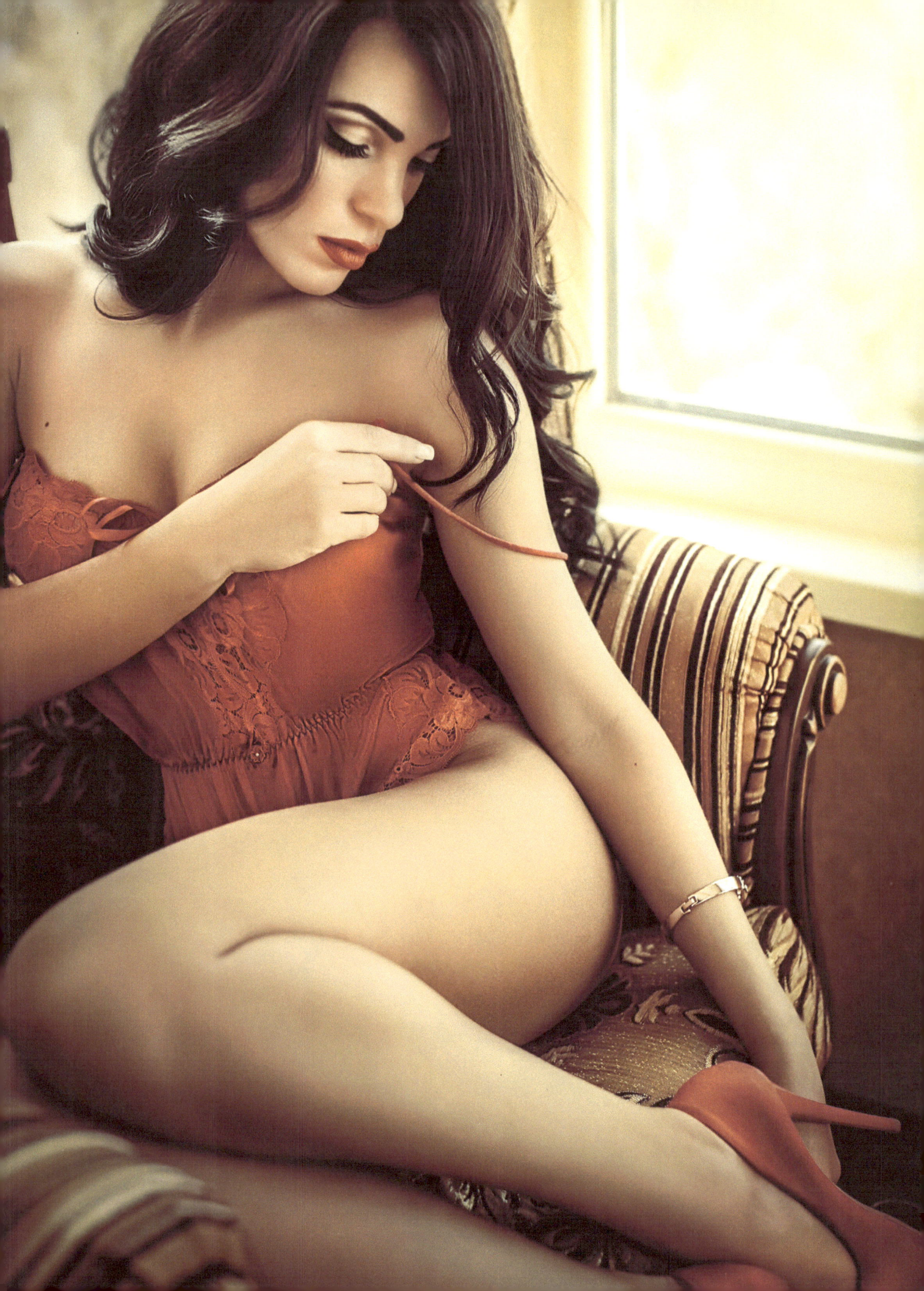

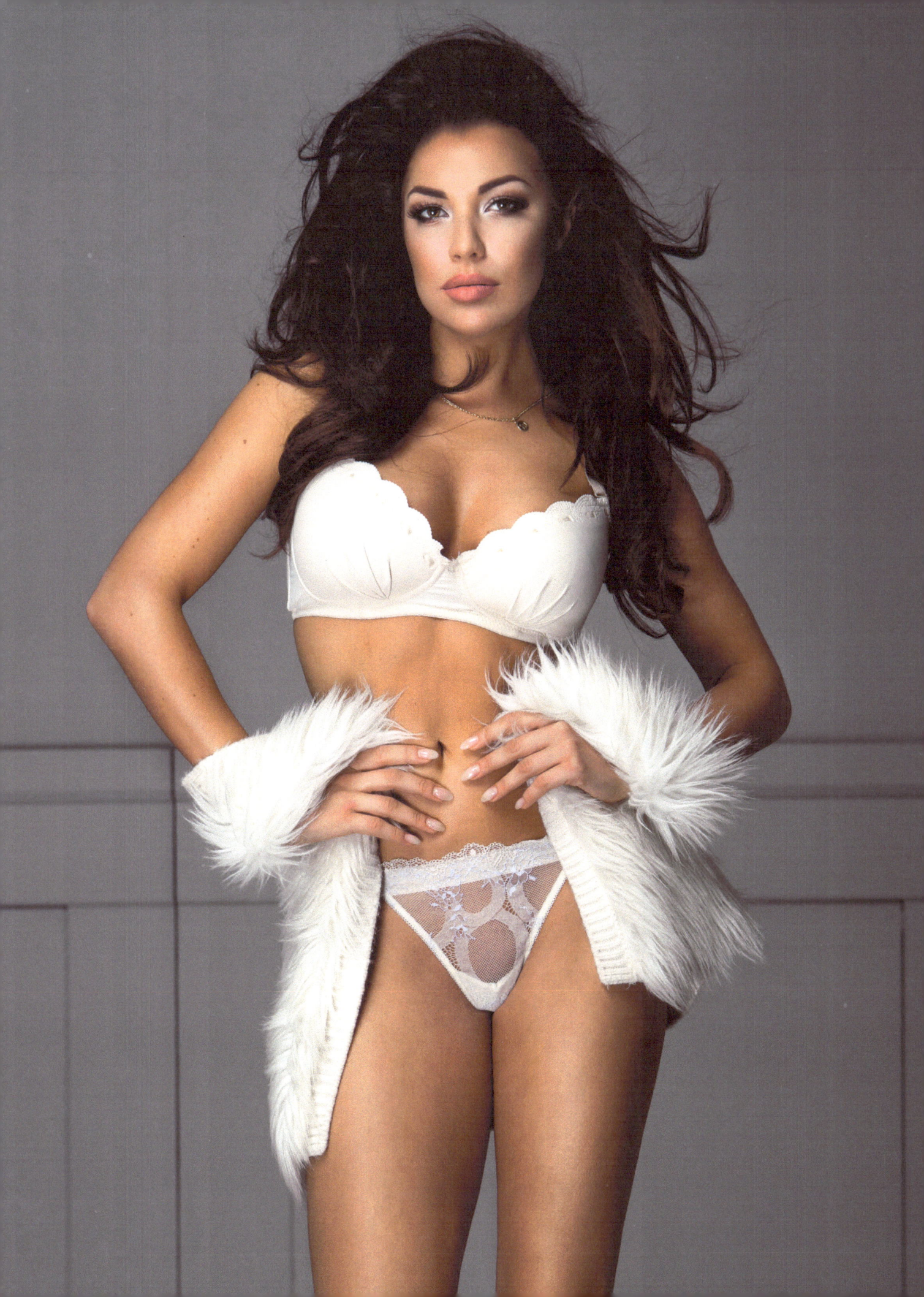

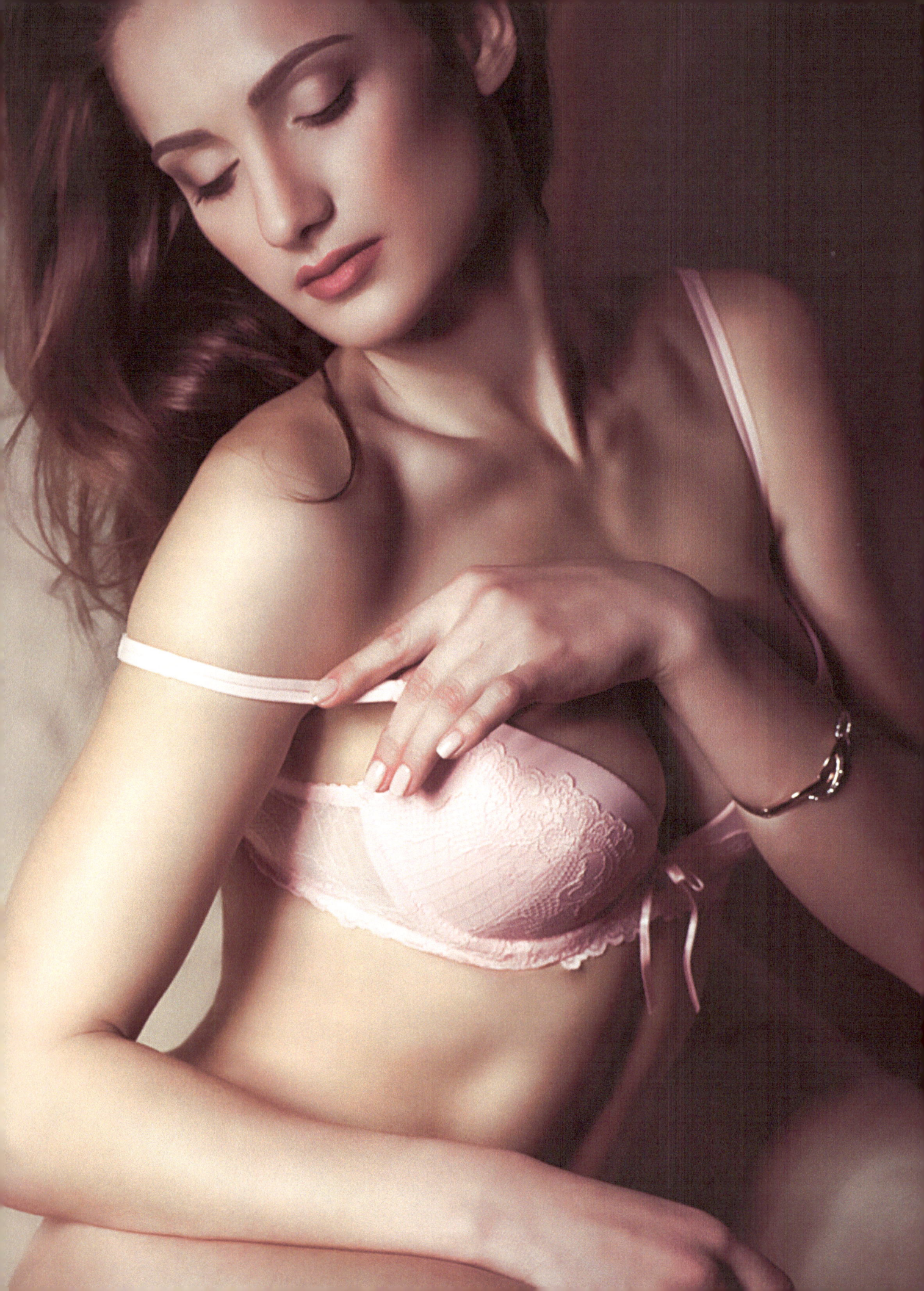

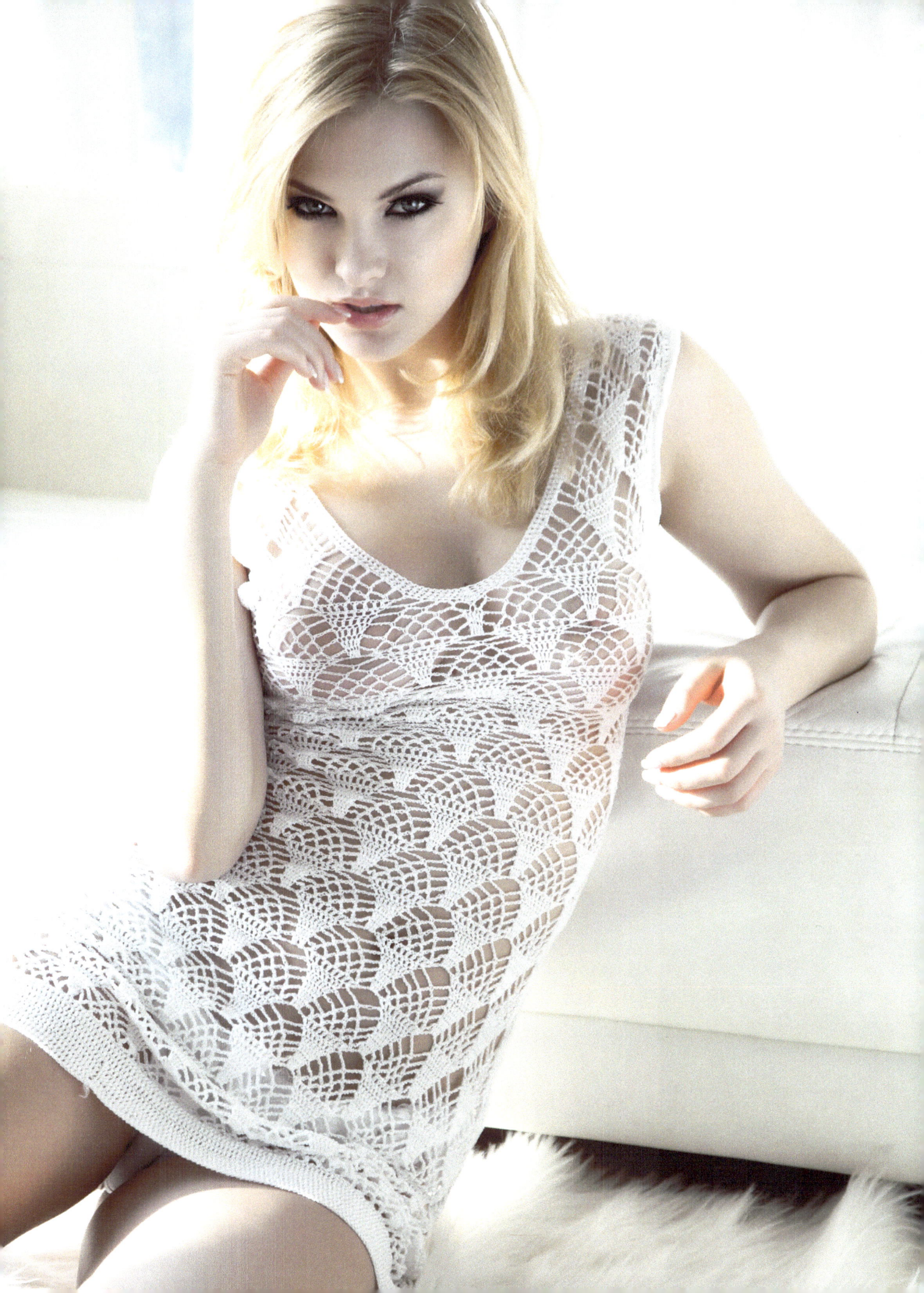

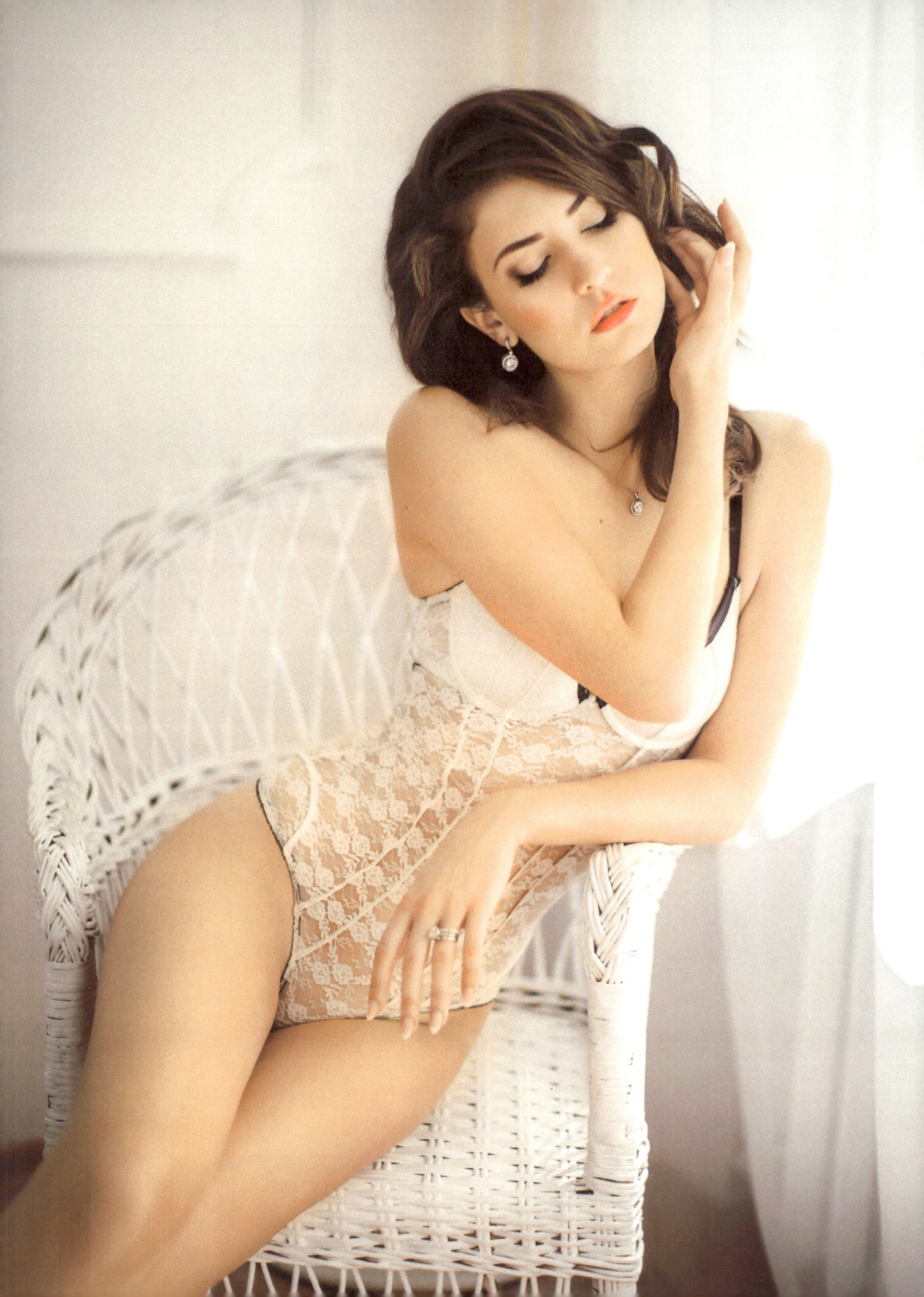

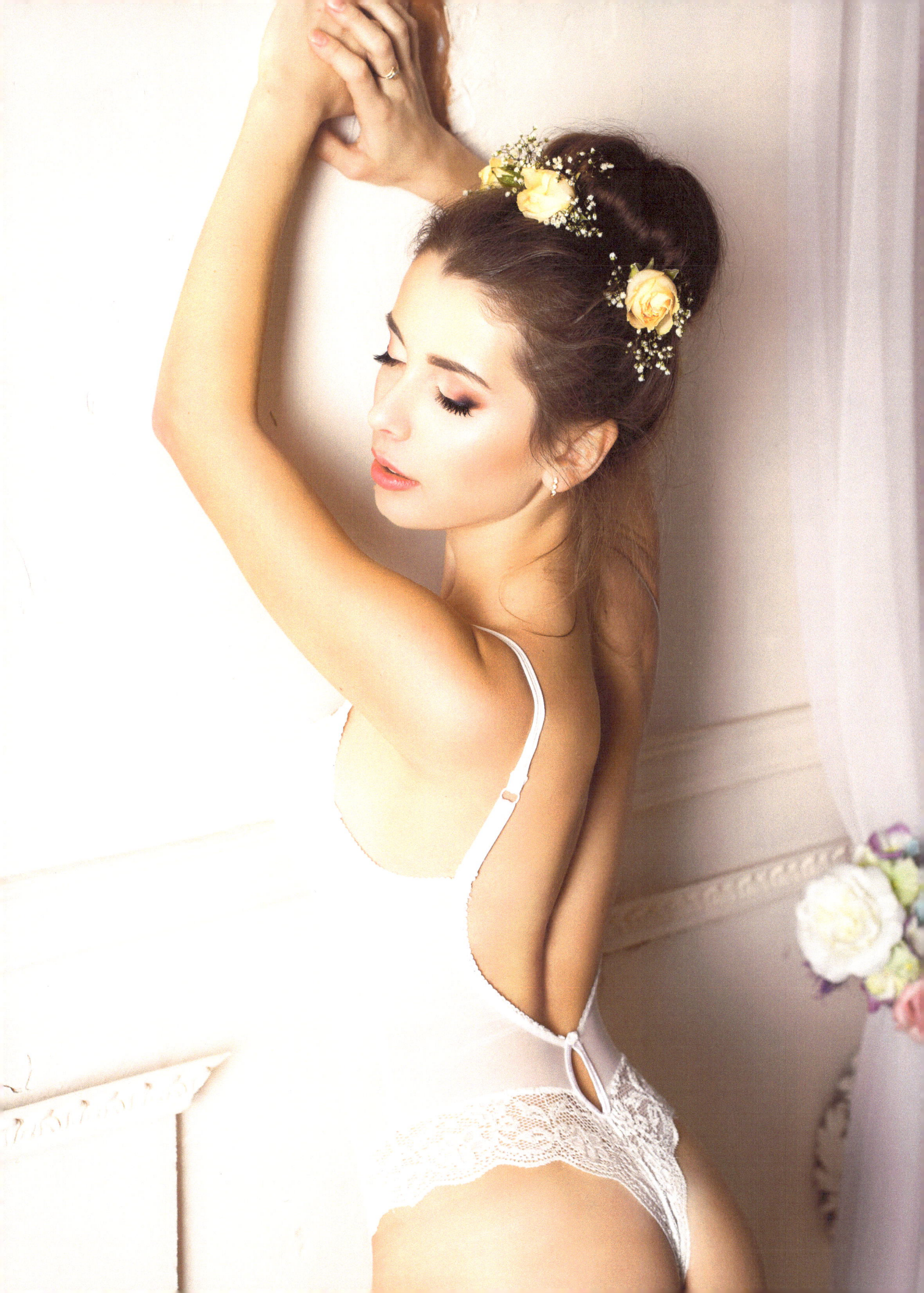

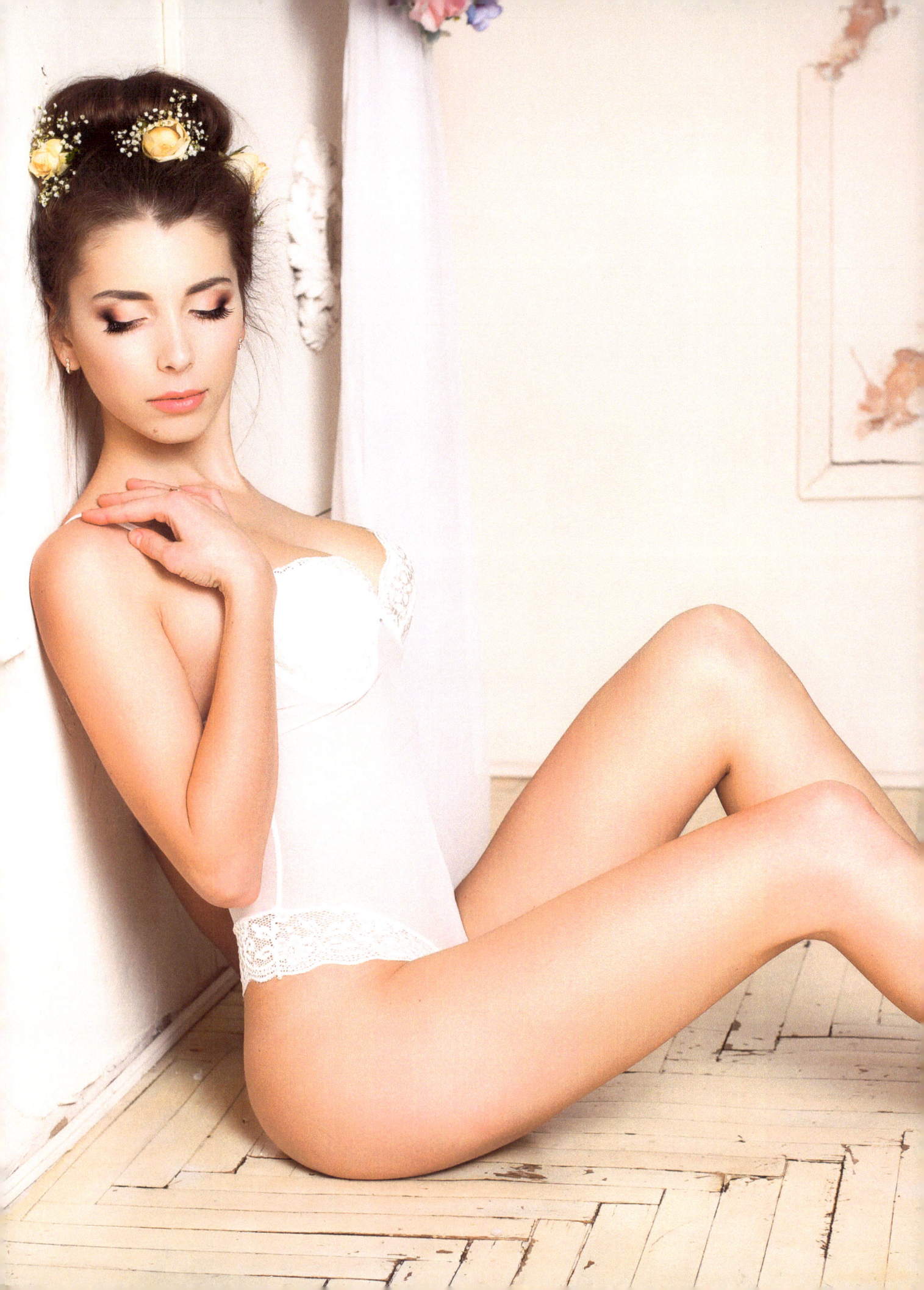

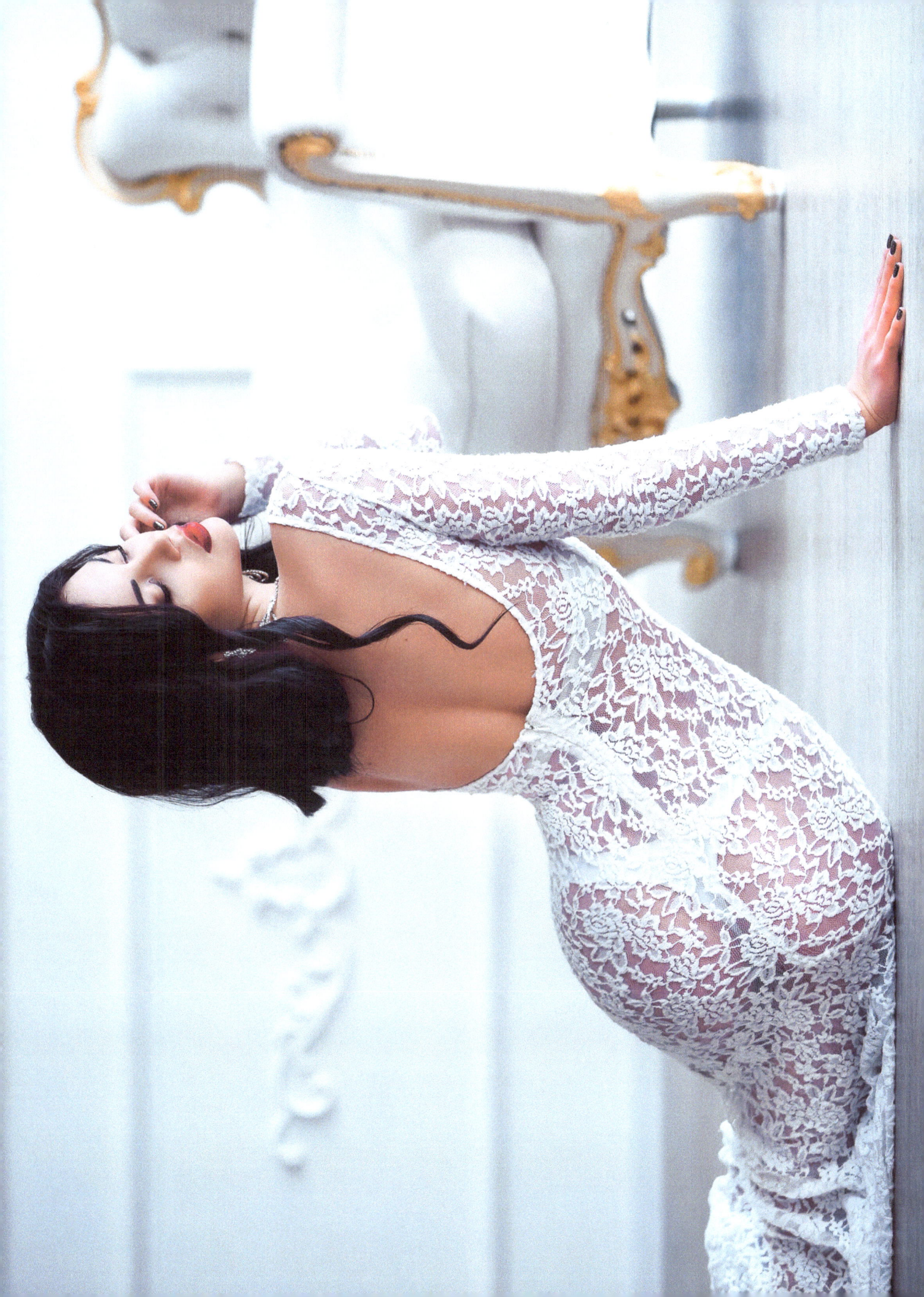

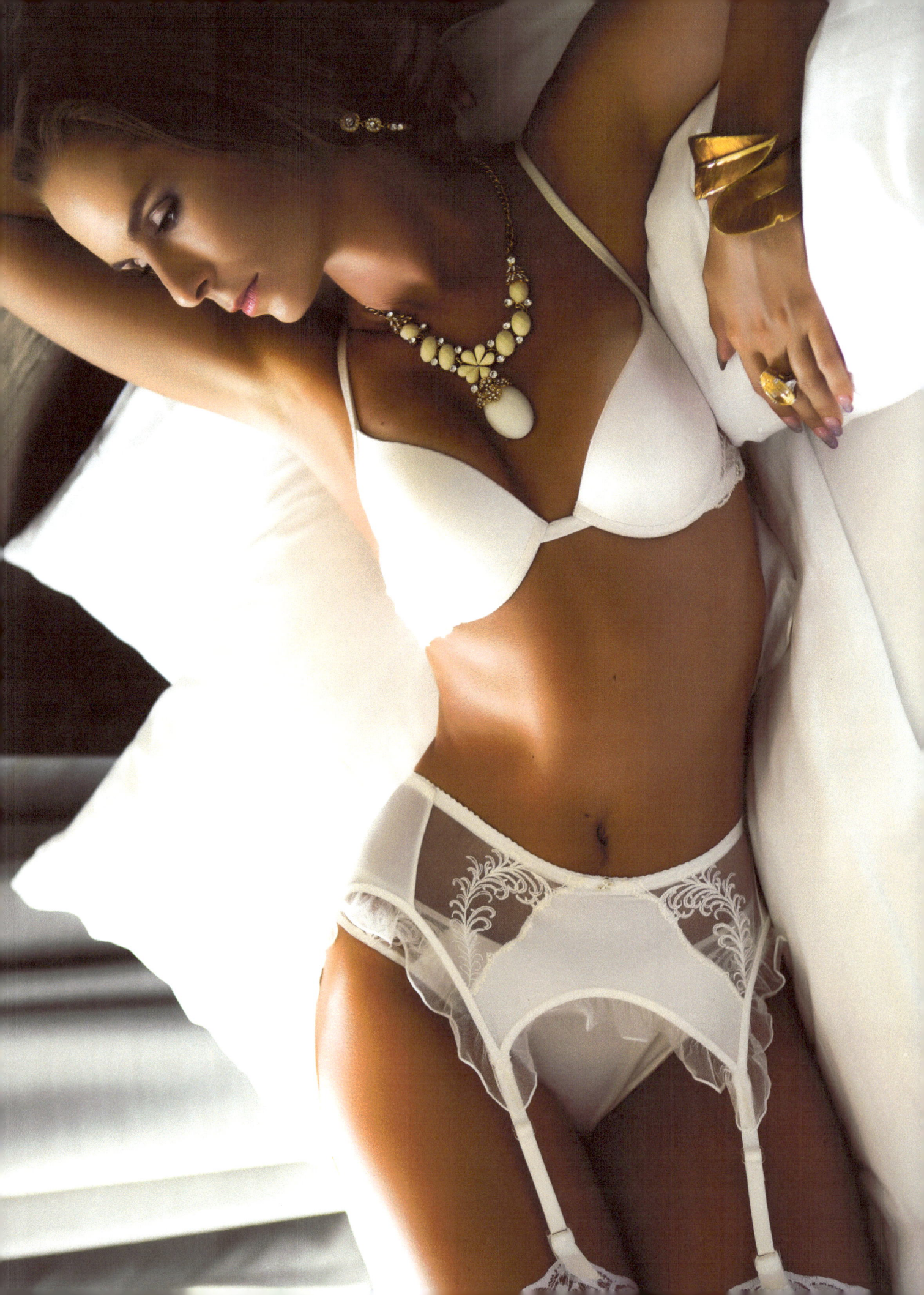

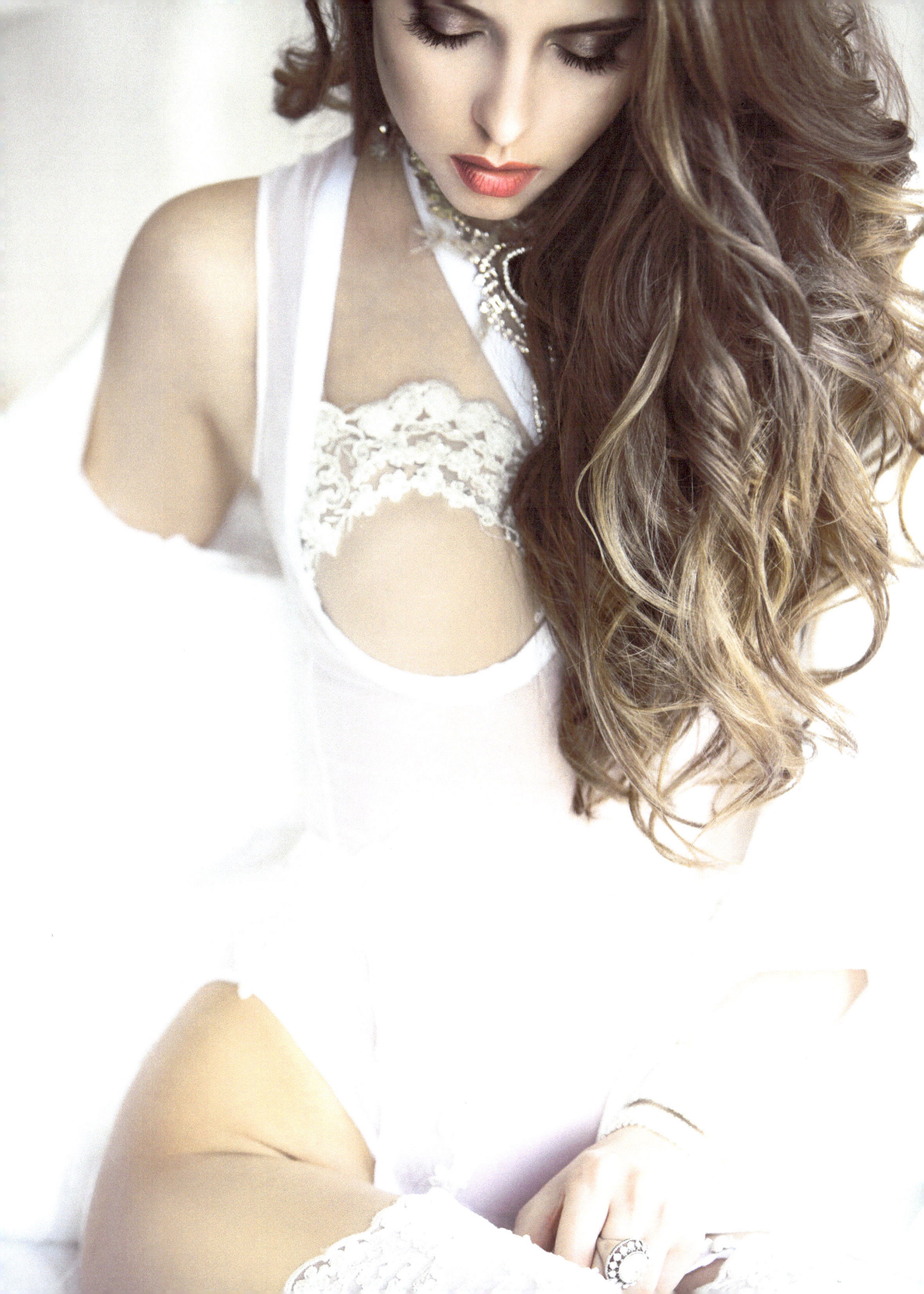

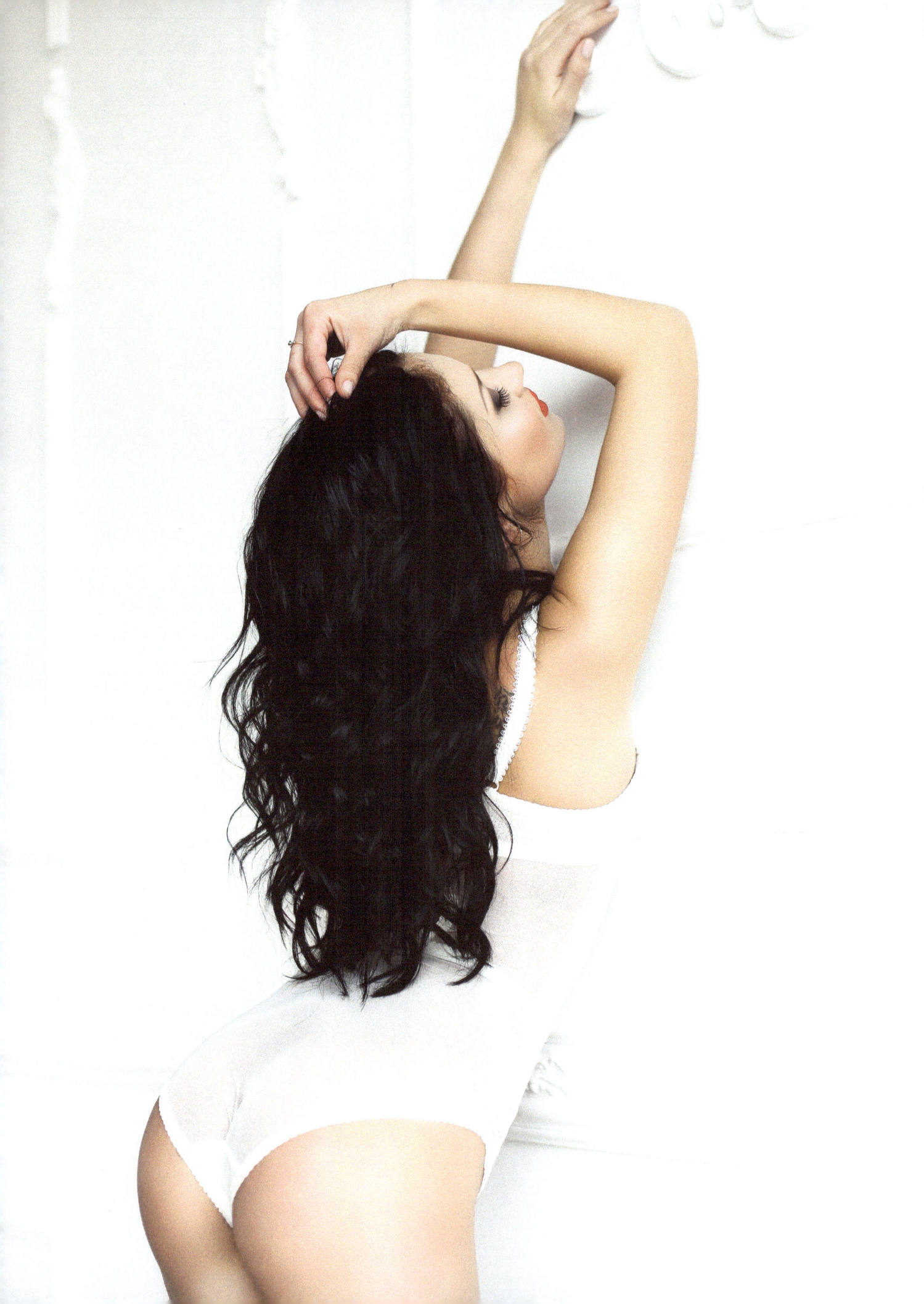

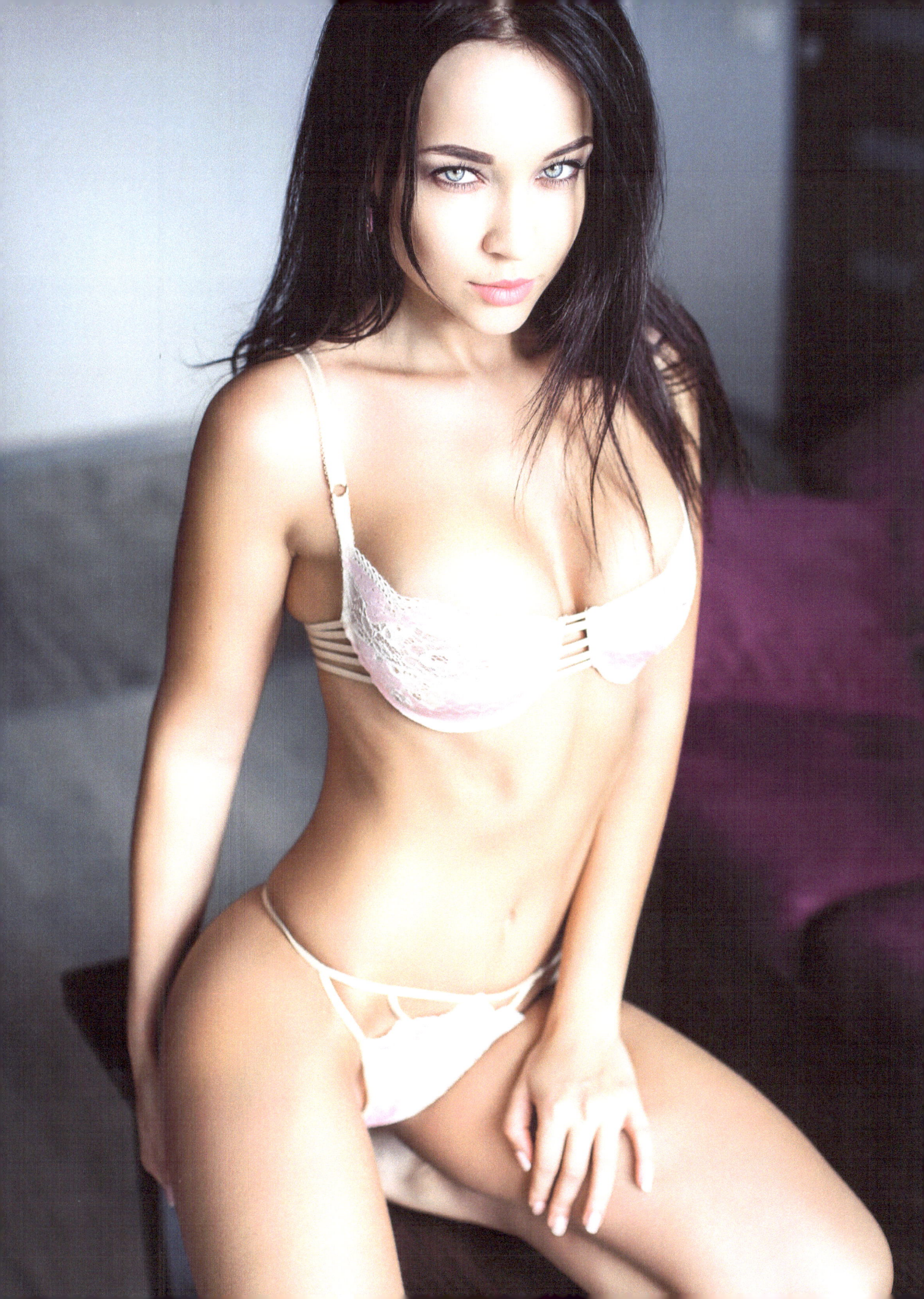

www.ingramcontent.com/pod-product-compliance
Lightning Source LLC
Chambersburg PA
CBHW050419180526
45159CB00005B/2327